Picture credits:
t=top b=bottom m=middle l=left r=right c=centre
FEMA News: 17bl, 18br, 39b, 40t
Andrea Booher/FEMA News: 10-11b, 15t
Michael Raphael/FEMA News: 13t
Jason Pack/FEMA News: 38t
Dave Saville/FEMA News: 38b
U.S. Geological Survey (USGS): 25t, 25b, 32t, 41t
National Oceanic and Atmospheric Administration (NOAA): 27t
World Food Programme (WFP): 30b
Digital Globe: 31b
National Aeronautics and Space Administration (NASA): 36t
Master Sgt Val Gempis/U.S. Air Force/Department of Defense (DoD): 39t

Copyright: Really Useful Map Company (HK) Ltd.
Published by: Robert Frederick Ltd.
4 North Parade Bath, England.
First Published: 2005

Designed and packaged by
Q2A Creative
Printed in China

FIRE & FLOOD

CONTENTS

Nature's Fury

Earthquakes, volcanic eruptions, storms, hurricanes, blizzards, fires and floods are all examples of natural disasters. Of these, fire and flood are probably the most common calamities to have plagued the world.

◄ *Lava flowing out of a volcano can set fire to forests and surrounding vegetation*

When the Earth trembles

Earthquakes are one of the main causes of fire. During an earthquake the ground trembles. A severe tremor can cause objects to be knocked down, and even lead huge buildings to crumble. In the event of an earthquake, a broken electric pole or a stove that has been knocked down is enough to start a fire.

Fire from beneath

Volcanoes too can cause fires. When a volcano erupts, it releases molten lava along with ash and mud. Lava is rock that has been melted due to the high temperatures inside the Earth's surface. When this liquid rock flows through towns and cities, the heat can set fire to the surrounding forests and houses.

Rising waters

Floods are usually caused by heavy rainfall, storms, or excessive melting of snow. Earthquakes and volcanoes cause floods in coastal regions. Floods can be accompanied by landslides. As the water loosens the mud, rocks and other debris on a hillside, these may start to slide down.

▶ *Heavy floods can sweep away trees, houses, vehicles and people*

▼ *Human activities like deforestation and fuel-burning are increasing the amount of greenhouse gases, leading to overheating of the Earth. This can cause heat waves, melting of glaciers, and a rise in sea levels – and result in fire and flood disasters*

Global warming

Global warming is a phenomenon whereby the Earth's temperatuure rises unnaturally. The root cause is enhanced 'greenhouse effect' – the trapping of heat in the Earth's atmosphere. The Earth radiates back part of the Sun's heat it receives. However, certain gases in the atmosphere, such as water vapour and carbon dioxide, prevent the heat from escaping into space. It is such greenhouse gases that have kept our planet warm.

Fire!

Fire is one of the most important discoveries in the history of mankind. It helps us cook food and keeps us warm during the long winters. However, if not handled carefully, fire can also wreak havoc. A fire that is out of control can be as dangerous as any other natural disaster, creating mass destruction of both life and property.

Fuelling the fire

Three elements are essential for a fire to survive – fuel, oxygen and heat. In forests, trees and other plants act as fuel. In buildings, the fuel source can be books, papers and furniture. Oxygen is a must for fire to survive. Also, the fire would die if there were no heat to sustain it. The flame emitted during a fire produces heat, which in turn heats the remaining fuel – making the fire grow stronger.

▲ *It is said that early man rubbed flintstones together to set fire to pieces of wood*

Heat

◄ *The fire triangle*

Oxygen　　　　**Fuel**

Gases and flames

Fire can be divided into four parts: fire gas, flame, heat and smoke. Certain poisonous gases like carbon monoxide are released during a fire. These are known as fire gases. Flame is the light that can be seen due to the burning of gas. Heat is the warmth that you feel while sitting next to a fire. But if you get too close, the heat can also burn you. A normal fire emits heat of about 1,100 degrees Celsius.

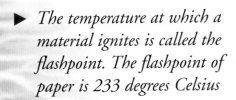

▶ *The temperature at which a material ignites is called the flashpoint. The flashpoint of paper is 233 degrees Celsius*

Smoke alarm!

Smoke is a harmful cloud of vapour mixed with powdered particles generated by a fire. A lot more people die by inhaling smoke and poisonous gases, than from actual burns.

Up in flames

Fire can be caused by human negligence or by natural forces like lightning, droughts, earthquakes and volcanoes. A huge fire that burns down towns and cities is known as a conflagration. Firestorms are huge fires produced by several separate fires burning at the same time.

▼ *Uncontrolled fires can reach temperatures as high as 1,500 degrees Celsius*

Forests on Fire

Wildfires, also known as forest fires, occur in natural settings like forests, woods and grasslands. They usually occur in places that experience long periods of hot, dry weather. These places also have a sufficiently moist climate to support the growth of trees and vegetation. Wildfires rage through thousands of acres of land within minutes, destroying everything in their path.

Spread like a wildfire

The spread of wildfires depends on the type and amount of fuel in the region. Fuel could be a piece of wood, logs, or even houses. The amount of material that can catch fire in a given area is called fuel load. The larger the fuel load, the faster the fire spreads.

▼ *Strong, gusty winds can help create a raging, uncontrollable fire*

▲ *Unless put out properly, embers from campfires can cause fire several days later*

Causes

Wildfires are sometimes caused by the heat of the Sun and lightning. However, most such fires are the result of human carelessness. Campfires not put out properly, and half-lit cigarettes or match-sticks can result in raging wildfires.

Half-lit cigarettes can unwittingly cause a forest fire

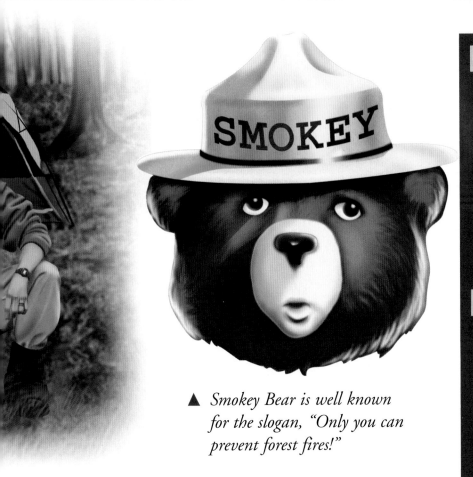

▲ *Smokey Bear is well known for the slogan, "Only you can prevent forest fires!"*

Good and bad fires

Wildfires can be classified as bad fires and good, or prescribed, fires. Prescribed fires are used to reduce the build-up of dry wood in forests, preventing potential wildfires. Experienced firefighters ensure that the fire does not spread to areas with human population. Bad fires, on the other hand, are uncontrolled wildfires.

Doctor's orders!

Wildfires are necessary to maintain the health of forests. Natural fires burn through the forest, consuming dry leaves and branches. Wildfires also encourage better growth of the natural vegetation by destroying unwanted plants, weeds and harmful pests.

Wildfires in History

Wildfires can be extremely destructive. Some of the worst wildfires in history have destroyed neighbouring towns and villages, killing thousands of people.

Peshtigo Fire

Considered to be one of the worst wildfires in American history, the Peshtigo Fire occurred on the same day as the Great Chicago Fire of 1871. The summer of 1871, being extremely dry, had witnessed the breakout of several small fires in the forests around Peshtigo. On October 8, strong winds added fuel to these fires, causing the wildfire to spread to about 12 towns.

Great Australian bushfire

In southeastern Australia, the extremely hot summer of 1983 made conditions perfect for bushfires. South Australia and Victoria had witnessed several small to moderate bushfires. However, no one was prepared for the devastation that was to hit on February 16, Ash Wednesday. A spate of bushfires spread through the region, killing 76 people and leaving over 2,400 families homeless.

The more a fire burns, the more fuel it can generate on its own — unless it is brought under control in good time

▲ *A scene of total devastation at San Bernardino County in southern California, following the 2003 forest fires*

Californian inferno

The fires that raged across southern California in October 2003 were perhaps the worst ever in the state's history. About 15 fires burned for two weeks in the counties of San Diego, Ventura, Riverside and San Bernardino, killing 24 people and destroying over 800,000 acres of land. The Cedar Fire of San Diego, with a casualty list of 14 people, was the largest in Californian records.

▼ *Trees such as the cedar can re-grow after being burned down in a fire, unless the seed too is destroyed*

European heat wave

In 2003, Europe witnessed some of the worst wildfires in its history, as a flaming inferno swept across the continent – from Portugal and Sweden, to far eastern Russia. France and Portugal were the worst hit. More than 22,000 acres of forests were destroyed in the south of France. In Portugal, over 500,000 acres of forests were destroyed in fires.

Battling Wildfires

▲ *Firefighters wear masks to protect themselves from smo*

Putting out wildfires not only requires special skills, but also calls for specific equipment. Besides the usual hazards, firefighters have to contend with wind speeds and sudden changes in the direction of the fire.

Equipment

Water-spraying trucks are the mainstay o ground crews. Crewmembers use a variety of equipment – from shovels and rakes, to a special tool called a pulaski. A combination of an axe and a mattock, the pulaski can be used to dig soil as well as chop wood. Firefighters wear special fire-resistant clothes to protect themselves from the blaze.

In the line of fire

Fire managers first assess the situation and plan a strategy to control the fire. Hotshots are responsible for building fire lines, or firebreaks, so the fire does not spread. They remove all flammable material along a strip around the wildfire. The fire is then suppressed by hotshot and engine crews. Helitack crews are trained in the use of helicopters for containing fires. Smokejumpers parachute from planes to fight wildfires in places not otherwise reachable.

◀ *The pulaski is named after its inventor, Ed Pulaski, who was a ranger with the United States Forest Service*

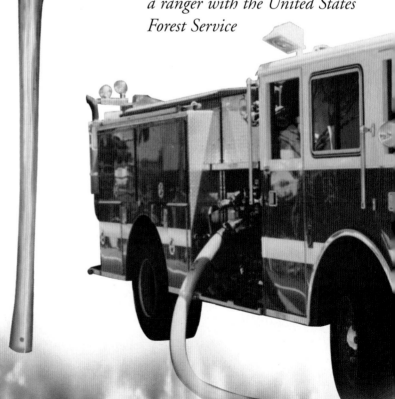

▲ *A helicopter spraying water to control a wildfire*

Airborne fighting

Tanker trucks are mostly inadequate to control wildfires, since they cannot be driven through dense forests. In such situations, airborne firefighters support the ground crew. The aerial crew use portable water pumps to put out small fires. Both helicopters and fixed-wing aircraft are used in aerial firefighting. Helicopters may be fitted with tanks or carry buckets. The buckets are usually filled by being dipped in lakes or reservoirs.

◀ *A fixed-wing aircraft sprays fire retardant*

Fire retardants

Apart from water, firefighters also use special chemicals that are capable of slowing down the rate of burning. These chemicals, called retardants, are sprayed over a wildfire to put the flames out.

◀ *A tanker truck is about 9 metres (30 feet) long and may hold over 1,000 gallons of water*

Buildings on Fire

A fire can engulf a building within no time. If not controlled, not only can a fire destroy a whole building, it can also spread across the neighbourhood and perhaps burn an entire city down.

Fire hazards

The most common cause of fire in buildings is human negligence. Leaving flammable material like wood, paper and aerosol cans near a fireplace or a stove can trigger a fire. Fuel leakage, faulty electrical wiring and cooking accidents are some of the other causes. Many fires have also been started by half-lit cigarettes, candles kept near windows, and children playing with matches.

In high-rise building fires, ladder trucks are used to reach the top floors

Risks galore

Fires in the lower floors of skyscrapers tend to cause the most damage. These fires can spread easily through all levels of the building and block escape routes, like stairwells, and trap the people on the higher floors. That is why skyscrapers are built with many more precautions than required for other buildings.

◄ *A firefighter climbs the aerial ladder set against a skyscraper*

▲ *A master stream mounted on an aerial ladder can pump out larger quantities of water than the hand-held hose*

Fiery behaviour

As the fire heats up the air in an enclosed area, it causes all combustible material therein to burst into flames in a huge explosion. This is called a flashover. When all the oxygen in the area is used up, the fire begins to die. If, however, there is a fresh supply of oxygen from outside, the fire gases will explode. This is called a backdraft.

Fearsome backdrafts

When a raging fire is starved of oxygen, the flames will die out. However, if a source of oxygen is provided, maybe by a door or window, there will be combustion which can create a fierce explosion from the gases and smoke remaining. The fire can come flying back towards the source of oxygen, hence the name backdraft. You do not want to be in the way of the backdraft!

Safety Precautions

▲ *A smoke alarm*

Fire is one of the most common disasters that threatens human life. Every year, hundreds of people die in fire accidents in buildings. Hence, most countries in the world have established certain standards that have to be met while constructing homes and Commercial centres.

▼ *Fire extinguishers commonly use water or foam to put out fires*

Fire alarms

Every building must have basic fire alarm systems in place. Smoke detectors are the most commonly used alarm systems. A shrill alarm goes off the moment smoke is detected, thus warning people of fire. Smoke detectors have to be tested every month, and batteries have to be changed on a yearly basis. Smoke detectors should also be replaced at least once in 10 years.

▼ *A fire hydrant should be placed at an accessible point in every neighbourhood*

Fire extinguishers

Portable fire extinguishers are a must for all buildings. It is the easiest way to control small fires and stop them from spreading. Alternatively, a good, long hose should be available to put out small fires. Most large buildings have water sprinklers in place. These sprinklers are automatically activated in case of fire, thus preventing it from spreading.

Building it safe

Modern buildings, especially skyscrapers, are made of strong, fire-resistant materials. They are equipped with extremely sensitive water sprinklers and enclosed stairwells, which ensure that fire is confined to rooms. Buildings should also have floor plans and evacuation procedures visible on every floor, to facilitate the orderly evacuation of people in the building and thereby also avoid a stampede during an emergency.

Be prepared

It is important to have an escape plan. Most building authorities hold fire drills to make sure that everyone knows what to do during a fire. Ideally there should always be two quick and safe escape routes chalked out. That way even if one of them is blocked, people can make it out into safety through the other.

▲ *Modern high-rise buildings, such as the Shanghai World Financial Centre, are built with unique fire-protection devices*

▶ *When climbing down an iron fire escape, one should be sure that there is no fire raging below. These escapes, though, are not common today*

Dos and Don'ts

In case of emergency, there are certain guidelines to be followed. Being thorough with these will not only ensure your safety, but also help to save others.

- Never ignore a fire alarm. It is always better to be safe than sorry

- Stay calm and make a quick exit from the building

- If you are in a high-rise building, exit in an orderly manner. Panic results in stampede and may cause more fatalities

- Take the stairs during a fire. You could get trapped in an elevator

- Stay close to the ground while escaping. Always remember that smoke rises, so you will find cleaner air near the ground

- Always test a door for heat before opening it. Touch the doorknob with the back of your hand. If it is hot, do not open the door. Look for an alternative route to escape

- Do not forget to close the door behind once you have exited a room. This helps delay the spread of fire

- If your clothing catches fire, roll on the ground to put it out

- Once you have exited the building, call the fire department immediately – in case no one has done so already

Here are a few things you can do if trapped in a room with no way to escape:

- First seal the opening under the door with wet towels. This will keep the smoke out
- If there is a phone in the room, call the emergency number or fire department and inform them of your whereabouts
- Stand near a window and signal for help
- Do not open the window unless you are sure that there is no fire below it

FACT FILE

CAUSES OF DOMESTIC FIRES IN ENGLAND AND WALES
- Cooking accidents: 54 per cent
- Heating appliances: 9 per cent
- Electrical appliances or wiring: 8 per cent
- Arson: 5 per cent
- Candles: 5 per cent
- Matches and cigarettes: 5 per cent
- Children playing with fire: 4 per cent
- Other causes: 11 per cent

▼ *It is particularly crucial to conduct regular fire drills with children, so they are familiar with escape routes during emergencies*

FIRE SYMBOLS

In case of fire

DO NOT use lift

Use the stairs

Call the Fire Department

The fire department consists of dedicated firefighters who take various risks to save thousands of others. Firefighting involves more than just putting out the fire. It also includes assessing the nature of the fire, the kind of fuel involved, and finding and rescuing people.

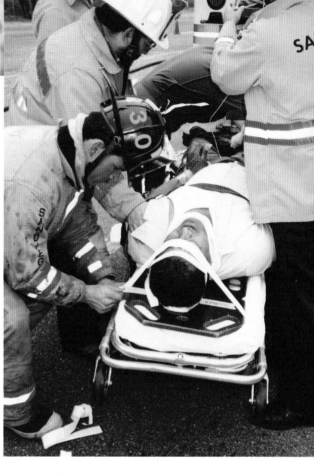

▲ *Firefighters give first-aid treatment to people they rescue*

To the rescue

When firefighters arrive at the scene, they make a quick assessment of the situation and proceed to evacuate people from the building or area. Sometimes they have to locate trapped people or animals. Firefighters work in teams. They wear fire-resistant clothes and breathing masks to safeguard against smoke and other poisonous gases.

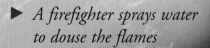

► *A firefighter sprays water to douse the flames*

Fighting with water

Water is most commonly used to put out fires. Wetting agents called detergents help water to penetrate objects such as mattresses. But flammable liquids like oil and petroleum float on water and help fire spread easily. In these situations, the fire is put out using foam.

▲ *Fire engines are equipped with various tools such as hoses, ladders and pike poles, as well as a water tanker*

Tools of life

Fire trucks include tanker, pumper and ladder trucks. Tankers can carry more water than pumpers. Ladder trucks have long ladders that help firefighters to reach the upper floors of tall buildings. Equipment such as ropes, axes and hoses are commonly used. Firefighters also carry extrication tools like spreaders and cutters to pull out trapped people.

Forever on call

Firefighters also play an important role when other natural disasters like floods and earthquakes strike. They help during road and rail accidents, and plane crashes as well.

▼ *Firefighters at the scene of a motor vehicle accident*

Towns on Fire

Sometimes, a small fire that started in a house or a barn is enough to burn down a whole city. Many such instances of a fire destroying an entire city are recorded in history.

Great Fire of London

The Great Fire of 1666 destroyed almost every public building in London. The fire broke out at the house of Thomas Farrinor, a baker to King Charles II. It is related that Farrinor forgot to put out his oven before going to bed. Sometime later, the embers from the oven set fire to some nearby wood. Aided by a strong wind, the fire spread across the neighbourhood.

▶ *The present St Paul's Cathedral in London was designed by architect Christopher Wren after the original one was burned in the 1666 fire*

▼ *The Great Chicago Fire of 1871 is believed to have started in a barn*

Great Chicago Fire

According to a popular legend, the fire that devastated Chicago in 1871 started in a barn owned by Kate O'Leary, when her cow kicked over a lantern. However, it is now believed that the fire was started by Daniel Sullivan, who had first reported it. Sullivan is said to have accidentally knocked over the lantern while trying to steal milk from Mrs. O'Leary's barn.

▲ *A view of the fire that raged through San Francisco following the earthquake of 1906*

Fire in San Francisco

Soon after a devastating earthquake rocked San Francisco on the morning of April 18, 1906, over 50 separate fires broke out. The quake had led to leakage in the main gas lines, causing the flare-ups. The fires were finally doused by dynamiting buildings to create firebreaks.

Tokyo in flames

On September 1, 1923, an earthquake measuring 7.9 on the Richter scale struck the Japanese island of Honshu. The quake destroyed Yokohama, a port city, along with the surrounding areas of Chiba, Kanagawa, Shizuoka and Tokyo. Most of the over 105,000 deaths were caused by 88 fires that broke out after the quake.

FACT FILE

OTHER MAJOR TOWN FIRES
- **1204:** Constantinople burns thrice during the Fourth Crusade (war fought to capture the Holy Land of Jerusalem from the Muslims)
- **1702:** Fire in Uppsala, Sweden, destroys a major part of the city, including the cathedral and Uppsala Castle
- **1889:** The Great Fire of Seattle devastates the entire city. All railroad terminals and most of the wharves are destroyed. Fortunately, no one is killed
- **1947:** Texas City Disaster; two ships carrying ammonium nitrate explode, causing massive destruction to the port and killing over 450 people – with another 100 declared as 'missing'

▼ *Tokyo was completely devastated by the Great Kanto Earthquake and the ensuing fire*

Fire Timeline

Despite the fact that fire can be controlled, we are rendered helpless in the face of a raging blaze. History is full of incidents in which fires have engulfed buildings and cities.

History in flames

Some of the biggest building fires occurred during ancient times. Most of these disasters were caused by humans. The famed Temple of Artemis at Ephesus, in modern-day Turkey, was one such casualty. Dedicated to Artemis, the Greek goddess of hunting, the temple was one of the Seven Wonders of the World. On the night of July 21, 356 BC, a young Greek named Herostratus set fire to the temple. Legend has it that Herostratus committed the crime to become famous.

▲ *It was Publius Cornelius Tacitus, the Roman historian, who started the myth that Nero 'played the fiddle' as he watched Rome burn*

Great Fire of Rome

On July 18, AD 64, a conflagration engulfed the city of Rome. The fire started among a few clustered shops and spread quickly through the streets. More than half the city was destroyed. Emperor Nero, the ruler of Rome at the time, was not in the city during the fire – giving rise to the famous rumour that Nero 'played the fiddle' while he watched Rome burn.

▶ *The 1945 atomic bombing produced a mushroom-like cloud formation over Hiroshima and Nagasaki*

In 1991, following the Persian Gulf War, the defeated Iraqi armed forces set fire to several of Kuwait's oil wells before retreating. The fires burned for several months

The Halifax explosion

On December 6, 1917, a French ship, *Mont Blanc*, and a Norwegian ship, *Imo*, collided in the harbour near Halifax, Nova Scotia, Canada. A fire started on-board the *Mont Blanc*, which was carrying a huge amount of ammunition to Europe for World War I. A few minutes later, a massive explosion took place, killing more than 1,600 people. About half of the town was wiped out.

The atomic bomb

On August 6, 1945, the first atomic bomb was dropped on the unsuspecting people of Hiroshima, Japan. Over 70,000 people were killed outright or shortly after the blast. A firestorm swept through the city immediately after, claiming more lives. Three days later, the second atomic bomb was dropped on Japan – this time on Nagasaki. About 40,000 people were reported to have died almost instantly. Several fires broke out, burning down houses and commercial buildings.

River Floods

Like fire, water also has the power to destroy lives and property. When water levels rise faster than the ground can absorb, flooding occurs. Floods can sweep away houses, trees and cars, and even drown people.

Causes

Floods can be caused by heavy rains, melting snow, broken dams, hurricanes and underwater volcanic eruptions. Broadly speaking, floods are of two kinds – regular river and coastal floods and flash floods.

▼ *An overflowing river directly causes floods*

◀ *Torrential rains are one of the major causes of floods*

The river overflows

River floods are caused when rivers overflow. This can happen due to several reasons. Heavy rains, either seasonal or caused by severe storms, can fill rivers and streams with more water than they can hold. When this happens, the water flows over the banks. Continuous rainfall can eventually cause water levels to rise and lead to flooding.

▲ *A truck submerged in swelling waters*

Killer rivers

The largest river floods have been recorded in China, where the Yangtze River has flooded almost every second year in the last 2,000 years. But it is the Hwang Ho (Yellow River) – also dubbed as 'China's Sorrow' – that has been responsible for more deaths than any other river in the world. The 1887 floods alone killed almost two million people.

Gift of the Nile

Not all river floods are destructive. For thousands of years, the Egyptians benefited from the flooding of the Nile. Every summer, when the mountain snow melted, the Nile flooded its banks – leaving behind black soil suitable for agriculture.

INTERESTING FACT

In 1970, the Aswan High Dam was built across the Nile to stop the river's annual flooding, so that farmers could plant crops through the year. Unfortunately, though, the dam has also prevented rich soil from being deposited on the riverbanks. As a result, farmers have had to resort to artificial fertilisers.

FACT FILE

OTHER MAJOR FLOODS
- **1931:** Hwang Ho; 850,000-4,000,000 people dead
- **1953:** North Sea; about 2,000 dead in the Netherlands and the United Kingdom
- **1975:** Typhoon strikes Henan Province in China, destroying more than 60 dams and causing floods; over 200,000 killed
- **2000:** Mozambique flood; thousands killed and millions rendered homeless
- **2002:** European flood; also called the 'flood of the century', it engulfs several countries including Russia, Germany, Poland and the Czech Republic; over 100 people killed

▼ *The soil deposited by the river Nile was very fertile. Hence, the annual flooding of the river was called the 'Gift of the Nile'!*

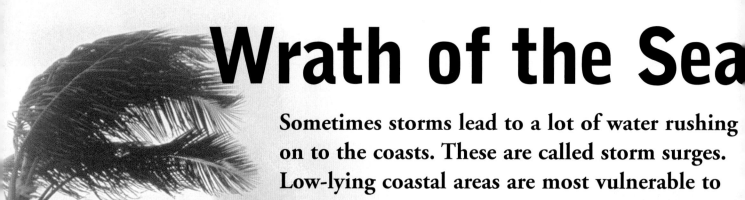

Wrath of the Sea

Sometimes storms lead to a lot of water rushing on to the coasts. These are called storm surges. Low-lying coastal areas are most vulnerable to storm surges.

▲ *The strong, whirling winds of a hurricane can cause huge waves in sea waters and flood coastal areas*

When the wind blows

One of the most common factors that affect sea levels is a hurricane. The storm makes the ocean surface fiercer than usual. Strong winds can create monstrous waves that crash on the beach, destroying houses and sometimes killing people. Storm surges are intensified by high tide and the direction in which the wind blows.

▼ *People in Bangladesh brave the flood waters to crowd outside a relief camp for food*

Hurricane menace

The worst storm surges in history have occurred in Bangladesh. In 1970, about 500,000 people were killed in a cyclone and accompanying storm surge. In 1991, about half of the country was flooded and over 139,000 killed in a devastating cyclone followed by huge storm surges.

Killer waves

Underwater volcanoes and earthquakes can create giant waves that are capable of travelling long distances at very high speeds. These waves, called tsunamis, can be more than 15 metres (50 feet) high and cause heavy destruction when they crash against the coast. The force of these killer waves can sweep away people, vehicles and huge buildings.

▶ *Tsunamis are very powerful waves and can cause extensive damage*

Asian tragedy

On December 26, 2004, an underwater earthquake occurred near the Indonesian island of Sumatra. The event generated a tsunami that went on to wreak havoc across eight countries, with over 10 others suffering various extents of damage. The most affected were Indonesia, Sri Lanka, South India and Thailand. The effects of the killer waves were felt as far as Port Elizabeth in South Africa. About 300,000 people have been reported dead.

▼ *A scene of the devastating Asian tsunami as it strikes the coastal areas of Sri Lanka*

Flash Floods

Flash floods are a sudden and unexpected surge of water. They are faster and more dangerous than normal floods. Like normal floods, though, flash floods too are caused by tropical storms, dam failures, heavy rains and rapid melting of snow.

Melting glaciers

When snow in nearby mountains starts melting at a very fast pace, it can lead to flash floods. Heat waves are usually the reason for rapid melting of snow. The water fills the streams, which are unable to hold the excess water, causing floods.

▲ *The tremendous volume and flow of water released by a dam break can cause much damage*

When a dam breaks

A breach in the dam is usually unpredictable and can happen within minutes. This lets out a huge amount of water, which surges downstream causing immense destruction. Reasons for dam failures can be poor design, bad construction, poor maintenance, or cracks caused by natural disasters like earthquakes.

▼ *The heat from the 1966 eruption of the Redoubt Volcano in Cook Inlet, Alaska, led to the rapid melting of ice in the vicinity – causing flash floods in the Drift River Valley below*

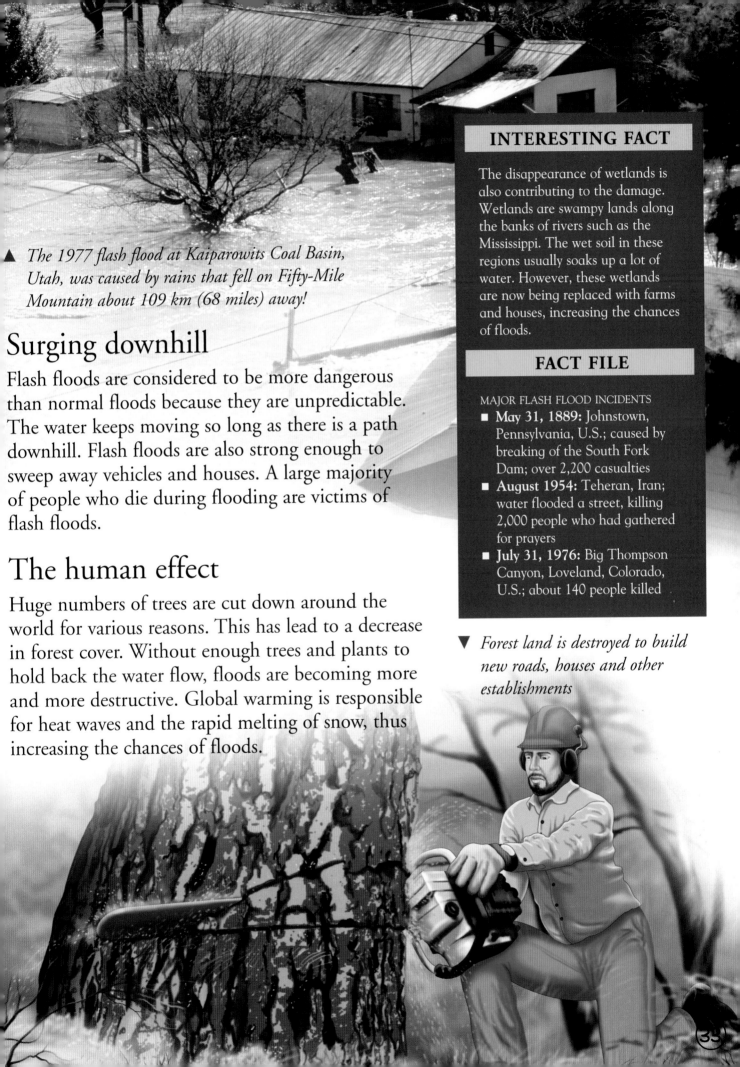

▲ *The 1977 flash flood at Kaiparowits Coal Basin, Utah, was caused by rains that fell on Fifty-Mile Mountain about 109 km (68 miles) away!*

Surging downhill

Flash floods are considered to be more dangerous than normal floods because they are unpredictable. The water keeps moving so long as there is a path downhill. Flash floods are also strong enough to sweep away vehicles and houses. A large majority of people who die during flooding are victims of flash floods.

The human effect

Huge numbers of trees are cut down around the world for various reasons. This has lead to a decrease in forest cover. Without enough trees and plants to hold back the water flow, floods are becoming more and more destructive. Global warming is responsible for heat waves and the rapid melting of snow, thus increasing the chances of floods.

INTERESTING FACT

The disappearance of wetlands is also contributing to the damage. Wetlands are swampy lands along the banks of rivers such as the Mississippi. The wet soil in these regions usually soaks up a lot of water. However, these wetlands are now being replaced with farms and houses, increasing the chances of floods.

FACT FILE

MAJOR FLASH FLOOD INCIDENTS
- **May 31, 1889:** Johnstown, Pennsylvania, U.S.; caused by breaking of the South Fork Dam; over 2,200 casualties
- **August 1954:** Teheran, Iran; water flooded a street, killing 2,000 people who had gathered for prayers
- **July 31, 1976:** Big Thompson Canyon, Loveland, Colorado, U.S.; about 140 people killed

▼ *Forest land is destroyed to build new roads, houses and other establishments*

Flood Contro

A common way to control floods is building dams across rivers. A chief factor for floods today is the effect of human activity on the environment. Planting trees will prevent soil erosion, and in turn help to contain floods. Preserving wetlands is another option.

▲ *The Thames Barrier has been raised more than 70 times since its construction was completed in 1982*

Putting up barriers

For years now, huge, sturdy dams have been constructed across rivers to control flooding. A reservoir, or artificial lake, constructed behind the dam stores the water, which is then supplied for irrigation and also used to produce electricity. Canals are dug to drain excess water.

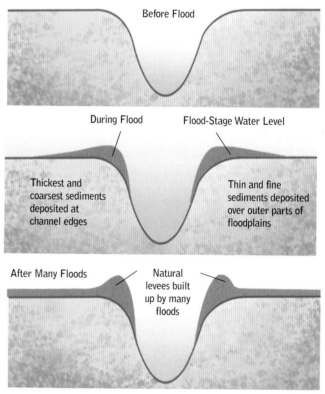

Before Flood

During Flood   Flood-Stage Water Level

Thickest and coarsest sediments deposited at channel edges

Thin and fine sediments deposited over outer parts of floodplains

After Many Floods   Natural levees built up by many floods

Levees

Apart from dams, levees and dikes are also used to prevent overflowing of river water. A levee is a slope that runs along a riverbank. It can be natural or manmade. Manmade levees are usually built by piling up mud from the bank. They are broad at the base and taper towards the top.

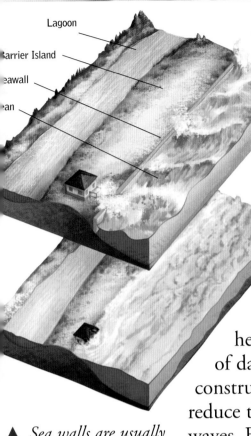

Lagoon
Barrier Island
Seawall
Ocean

Keeping the sea out

There is not much that man can do to stop a raging sea from destroying the shores. However, coastal defences like sea walls, dikes and beach nourishment help to reduce the extent of damage. Sea walls are constructed on the coast to reduce the effect of strong waves. Beach nourishment is the process by which sand lost by erosion is replaced.

▲ *Sea walls are usually made of concrete and may be vertical, sloping or curved*

▼ *Planting trees will prevent soil erosion, thus reducing the chances and effects of floods*

Dikes

Dikes are walls made of stone or baked clay built to defend an area from floods. Dikes can be permanent structures or just built during a flood emergency. They are also built to reclaim land from the sea. A series of dikes are built to keep the sea out and create new lands by draining the water in the area.

Flood Forecast

Unlike fire, floods are definitely more predictable. Over the years, early warnings and flood forecasts have helped to save several lives.

◀ *TIROS I was successfully used to survey atmospheric conditions from space*

Eyes in the sky

Weather satellites gather vital information and capture pictures of cloud formation above the Earth. These pictures help to predict thunderstorms, hurricanes and even flash floods. After the scientists collect enough data, it is communicated to people through televisions, radios and newspapers.

▶ *The water levels and the flow of river water are monitored by gauging stations like this one in Cowlitz County, Washington, U.S.*

Monitoring water levels

Most developed countries have river-monitoring and rainfall-measuring stations. Scientists in these stations keep a close watch on water levels and the amount of rain received in the region.

Gauging floods

Rain gauges are used to measure the amount of rainfall in a particular area. Scientists also use flow measurement equipment to monitor the speed of a river flow. Coastal flooding predictions are made in similar fashion to ones for river floods and flash floods. Special ocean monitoring stations and tsunami warning centres have also been set up to forewarn people in coastal areas.

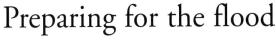

◄ *The markings on river stakes are monitored for rising water levels*

Preparing for the flood

The moment a warning is given out, turn off the main power supply and prepare to evacuate. If time is short for evacuation, move to higher ground. Avoid wading into floodwaters, since they are highly infectious and can spread diseases. Listen to the radio continuously for updates.

◄ *Always heed road signs and avoid storm drains. Also, keep away from blocked roads*

HIGH WATER

To the Rescue

The extent and focus of rescue and relief efforts depend upon the kind of flood. During flash floods, the emphasis is on saving lives; while in slow-moving river floods, preventing damage to property gains importance.

◀ *Swift-water rescue requires a lot of training and skill*

A tough battle

The members of a rescue team undergo strict training in water rescue, especially swift-water rescue. This comes in handy particularly during flash floods.

▼ *The local police are patrolling a flood-hit area. The local police and firefighters are always the first to arrive at a flood scene*

Tools for rescue

Boats are one of the most important tools of flood rescue. They are the only means of transportation during floods and, hence, are vital to rescue work. Flotation devices, ropes and safety lines come in very handy in rescue efforts. Rescuers wear helmets to protect their heads from rocks and logs that are swept along by the water. Sometimes, land rescuers are aided by helicopters and army personnel.

▲ *Relief measures in flood-affected areas include the supply of food and medicines*

The aftermath

Some of the worst effects of floods are felt after the water has receded. This is because floods are capable of spreading diseases. More people die due to epidemics that spread after a flood, so medical aid is of utmost importance. Floods also destroy crops, leading to starvation and poverty. In 1887, more than one million Chinese starved to death after a flood destroyed the crops.

Life after the flood

The rushing water can deposit a huge amount of mud, capable of burying everything. Houses can be swept away. Railroads, bridges and highways can be broken or washed away. Telephone lines can be destroyed, making communication impossible. Imagine having to rebuild after such enormous loss. But that is what people who live in flood-prone areas do every time a flood washes their world away.

▼ *In emergencies, helicopters are used to airlift people marooned by the rising waters in a flood*

Flood Timeline

Ever since prehistoric times, floods have been one of the biggest disasters to threaten man. More people are killed by floods than by fire. Let us take a look at some of the worst floods in recorded history.

▼ *Coastal habitations are more prone to be submerged in flood waters without prior warning*

English storms

England has witnessed some of the worst floods in history. The first recorded one to cause a great deal of damage to life and property occurred in 1099. High tides and storm surges flooded the English coast, killing nearly 100,000 people. In 1287, strong waves from the Zuider Zee claimed about 500 lives in East Anglia, England.

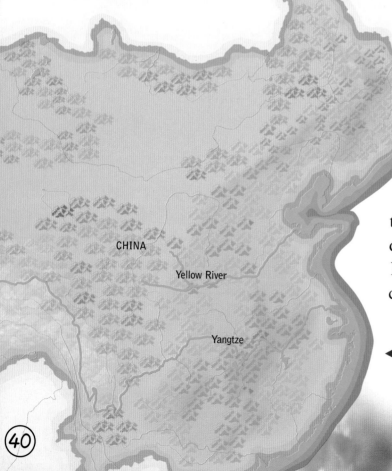

CHINA

Yellow River

Yangtze

Chinese jinx

The Yangtze and Yellow rivers in China are known for their life-threatening floods. In 1871, the Yangtze River was believed to have risen so high that, once the water receded, a boat was found stuck on a rock 37 metres (120 feet) above ground! In September 1887, the Yellow River flooded 300 villages – drowning about 900,000 people. In 1931, the Yellow River overflowed again, claiming about four million lives.

◀ *The Chinese have started construction of the Three Gorges Dam to control the Yangtze River. The Yellow River, however, continues to pose a serious threat to those who live on its banks*

▲ *Poor tenant farmers displaced by the great Mississippi flood of 1927 are stranded on the levees near the river*

Great floods of America

The United States is well known for its stormy coasts and flash floods. On May 31, 1889, the South Fork Dam in Johnstown, Pennsylvania, broke and immediately caused flash floods. Over 2,200 people were killed in what was considered as one of the worst disasters after the American Civil War (1861-65).

◄ *Every year, floods in Bangladesh threaten the lives and homes of thousands of people*

High tides in Bangladesh

Every year during monsoon, floods in Bangladesh claim hundreds of lives and leave millions homeless. One of the worst floods occurred in 1998, when more than half the country was submerged for three months. About 1,000 people lost their lives. The flood in 2004 was similarly devastating. More than 450 people died, while millions had to flee their homes.

Myths and Legends

Ancient people considered fire and flood disasters to be an expression of the anger of gods or Mother Nature. In many countries, people made human and animal sacrifices to appease the elements.

Discovery of fire

According to a Greek legend, Prometheus, who created man, wanted to gift his creation the warmth of fire. He went to Zeus with his request. Although Zeus turned him down, Prometheus was determined. He stole fire from the gods and gave it to mankind.

▶ *Zeus punished Prometheus, who had stolen fire, by chaining him to the Caucasus Mountain*

Hawaiian people attribute volcanic eruptions to Goddess Pele's anger

Fire gods

In many countries, fire gods are much feared and several disasters are attributed to their anger. This is most pronounced in Hawaii. According to the local legend, Pele, the goddess of fire, resides on Mauna Kea. She is regarded as the protector of the Hawaiian people. At the same time, she is feared for her violent temper. In Greek mythology, Hephaestus is worshipped as the god of fire, while Vulcan is the Roman equivalent of Hephaestus. In India, fire continues to be an important part of rituals in the Hindu religion.

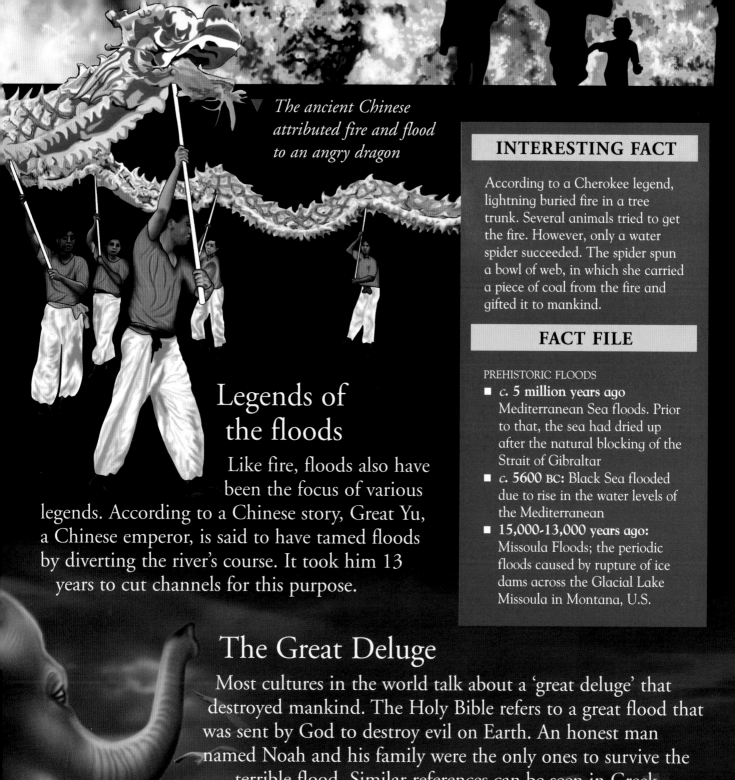

The ancient Chinese attributed fire and flood to an angry dragon

Legends of the floods

Like fire, floods also have been the focus of various legends. According to a Chinese story, Great Yu, a Chinese emperor, is said to have tamed floods by diverting the river's course. It took him 13 years to cut channels for this purpose.

The Great Deluge

Most cultures in the world talk about a 'great deluge' that destroyed mankind. The Holy Bible refers to a great flood that was sent by God to destroy evil on Earth. An honest man named Noah and his family were the only ones to survive the terrible flood. Similar references can be seen in Greek, Roman, Indian, Chinese and Scandinavian mythology.

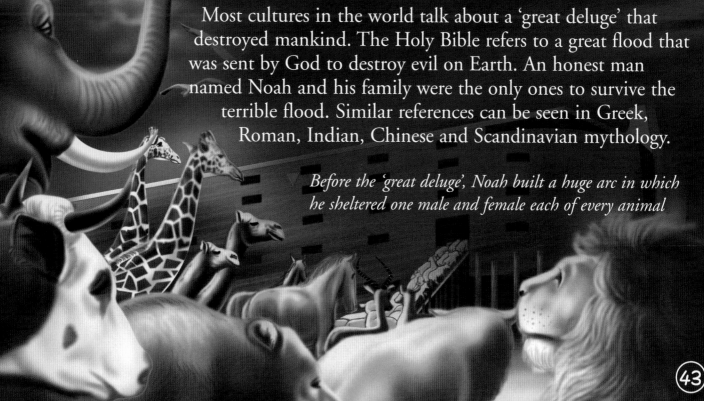

Before the 'great deluge', Noah built a huge arc in which he sheltered one male and female each of every animal

Glossary

Aerosol: A substance – such as insecticide, paint or perfume – packaged under pressure for release as a spray of fine solid or liquid particles

Alternative: A choice between two or more possibilities

Ammunition: Material such as bullets, rockets or grenades that can be used as, or in, weapons

Blizzard: Violent snowstorm accompanied by heavy winds

Breach: An opening, a tear, or a crack

Bush fire: Wildfire in Australia

Casualty: One killed or injured in an accident or natural disaster

Catastrophe: A huge and sudden disaster or bad event

Cherokee: A Native American tribe; used to inhabit the southern Appalachian Mountains, between western Carolina and northern Georgia

Combustible: Capable of burning

Debris: Rubble, or scattered remains of something that is broken

Deforestation: Cutting down of trees on a large scale

Deluge: A huge flood. In biblical terms, the flood that occurred during Noah's time

Devastation: Complete or utter destruction

Douse: To put out, or to immerse in liquid

Downstream: In the direction that a stream or river flows

Ember: A small, glowing piece of coal found in a dying fire

Epidemic: Rapid spread of infectious disease, affecting several people in a particular area at the same time

Erosion: The process by which material, such as soil, is washed away from the Earth's surface

Evacuate: To remove or withdraw people from a certain area

Extrication: To remove, or release, from an entanglement

Fatality: Death caused by an accident or disaster

Fiddle: Violin

Fire extinguisher: A portable mechanical device used to spray water or chemicals into a fire to put it out

Flammable: Liable to catch fire; easily burned

Flintstone: A hard, blackish stone that produces fire when struck with steel

Forecast: To estimate or predict weather conditions in advance, using methods of scientific analysis

Fragment: Piece; small part that has been broken off from a bigger item

Habitat: The natural environment in which a particular organism or a community lives

Harbour: A sheltered part of a body of water – such as a river or a sea – deep enough to accommodate ships

High tide: The time when water in the sea reaches its highest level

Hurricane: A tropical storm accompanied by strong winds and causing heavy rains and widespread flooding

Ice dam: A natural mass of ice at the mouth of a river or lake acting as a barrier

Inferno: A place of fiery heat

Lava: Molten rock, or magma

Livestock: Farm animals raised for profit

Mattock: A digging tool with a flat blade

Monsoon: A wind system that brings heavy rainfall to a region

Portable: Something that can be carried around, like a portable stereo

Precaution: An action taken in advance to protect oneself against danger

Recede: Move back, or withdraw, from a point

Reclaim: To make suitable, or return to a suitable condition, for use

Reservoir: A natural or artificial pond or lake used to store water

Richter scale: Instrument used to measure the intensity of an earthquake

Stampede: A sudden, frenzied rush of panic-stricken people or animals

Storm drain: A storm sewer

Tremor: The shaking or trembling experienced during an earthquake

Wharve: A shore or a riverbank where ships are tied up for loading and unloading